Events of
1929

News for every day of the year

The *Graf Zeppelin* on its round the world flight.

By Hugh Morrison

MONTPELIER PUBLISHING
LONDON

Published in Great Britain by Montpelier Publishing, London.

Distributed by Amazon Createspace/KDP.

ISBN: 9781796493733

January 1929

Tuesday 1: German President Paul von Hindenburg demands that Allied occupation of the Rhineland, in place since 1918, should end.

Wednesday 2: Anton Korošec, Prime Minister of Yugoslavia, resigns over demands for Croatian autonomy.

Thursday 3: Filmmaker Sergio Leone (*The Good, The Bad and the Ugly, A Fistful of Dollars*) is born in Rome (died 1989).

Von Hindenburg.

Raphael's Madonna.

Friday 4: It is announced that US Treasury Secretary has bought Raphael's Niccolini-Cowper Madonna for $1m, the highest amount paid for a painting at that date.

Saturday 5: American countries sign the General Act of Inter-American Arbitration resolving to use peaceful means to end international disputes.

Sunday 6: Heinrich Himmler becomes supreme commander (*Reichsführer*) of the Nazi party's paramilitary force the *Schutzstaffel* (SS).

Heinrich Himmler.

January 1929

Monday 7: The US aircraft *Question Mark* sets a world record when it completes over 150 hours of non-stop flight using aerial refueling.

Question Mark refueling.

Tuesday 8: Actor Saeed Jaffrey OBE (*My Beautiful Laundrette, A Passage to India*) is born in Malerkotla, India. (Died 2015).

Wednesday 9: Yugoslavia bans public assemblies as the country slides into authoritarian rule.

Thursday 10: The cartoon character Tintin makes his first appearance, in the Belgian children's comic *Le Petit Vingtième.* He is thought to have been inspired by teenage travel writer Palle Huld.

Friday 11: The Soviet Union reduces the working day to seven hours.

Palle Huld, the inspiration for Tintin?

Saturday 12: Romantic adventure film *The Rescue* starring Ronald Colman and Lili Damita is released.

Sunday 13: Wild West legend Wyatt Earp dies aged 80.

Ronald Colman.

Wyatt Earp.

January 1929

Monday 14: The US Supreme Court rules in Wisconsin *v.* Illinois that federal law can be imposed on a state if it is carrying out actions which are harmful to another state.

Civil rights leader Martin Luther King, born 15 January.

Tuesday 15: Civil rights activist and clergyman Martin Luther King Jr is born in Atlanta, Georgia (assassinated 1968).

Wednesday 16: General Bramwell Booth, leader of the Salvation Army, is voted unfit to rule due to declining health and is forced to step down.

Thursday 17: The comic strip character Popeye the Sailor makes his first appearance in print.

Friday 18: British forces rescue Inayatullah Khan, the deposed King of Afghanistan, by air from Kabul.

Saturday 19: The Hawes-Cooper Act is passed in the USA, restricting the use of prison labour to undercut free market labour.

Sunday 20: Jazz legend Jimmy Cobb, drummer for Miles Davis, is born in Washington DC.

Inayatullah Khan, the deposed King of Afghanistan.

January 1929

Monday 21: Italian police destroy 2000 fake US passports in a clampdown on emigrants engaged in bootlegging.

Tuesday 22: The 'part talkie' film *Lady of the Pavements* directed by D.W. Griffith is released. It uses the Vitaphone system of gramophone disks for the sound sequences.

Left: Redskin premieres on 26 January.

Wednesday 23: 14 members of the Poona Horse cavalry regiment are killed during a friendly-fire incident in Peshawar, India.

Thursday 24: *The Seven Dials Mystery* by Agatha Christie is published.

Friday 25: Italy announces a major ship-building programme to bring its navy up to strength with other western powers.

Saturday 26: The film *Redskin* starring Richard Dix is released. Part of the film is shown in Technicolor and an early widescreen format, 'Magnascope'.

Admiral Byrd's memorial, Antarctica.

Sunday 27: Admiral Richard E. Byrd's US expedition to Antarctica discovers the Rockefeller Mountains and Washington Ridge.

January/February 1929

Monday 28: Outgoing US President Calvin Coolidge warns that American prosperity can only be maintained if rigid economical practice is observed.

Tuesday 29: Erich Maria Remarque's war novel *All Quiet On The Western Front* is published.

Wednesday 30: Former Moulin Rouge dancer *La Goulue* (Louise Weber), immortalised on canvas by Toulouse-Lautrec, dies destitute in Paris aged 73.

Thursday 31: Leon Trotsky is expelled from the Soviet Union and sent into exile.

Friday 1: 1600 supporters of Leon Trotsky are exiled to Siberia.

Saturday 2: Norway annexes Peter I Island in Antarctica.

Sunday 3: Martial law is declared in Valencia, Spain, as troops put down an anti-government revolt.

Toulouse Lautrec's model *La Goulue* **dies aged 73.**

February 1929

The Ford Model A.

Monday 4: The one millionth Ford Model A motor car is completed.

Tuesday 5: The General Electric Company makes a long-distance television broadcast, transmitting the face and voice of film director D.W.Griffith from Schnectady, NY, to Los Angeles.

Wednesday 6: Germany accepts the Kellogg-Briand Pact, resolving not to use war to settle international disputes.

Thursday 7: The US Federal Reserve Board issues a warning over excessive speculation in property, shares and loans.

Friday 8: Irish Free State politician and future President of the Republic of Ireland, Éamon de Valera, is sentenced to one month's imprisonment for entering Northern Ireland.

Saturday 9: Estonia, Latvia, Poland, Romania and the USSR sign Litvinov's Pact, renouncing war.

Sunday 10: Mexican President Emilio Portes Gil survives an assassination attempt when his train carriage is blown up.

February 1929

Monday 11: The Kingdom of Italy and the Roman Catholic church sign the Lateran Treaty, settling the 'Roman Question' over whether the church or state should govern Italy. The Vatican City becomes an independent state within Rome.

Tuesday 12: Lillie Langtry, British singer/actress and former mistress of the Prince of Wales (later King Edward VII), dies aged 75.

Wednesday 13: Outgoing US President Calvin Coolidge signs a naval bill for the construction of 15 new cruisers and an aircraft carrier.

Lily Langtry, shown here in 1885, dies on 12 February.

Thursday 14: The 'Saint Valentine's Day Massacre' takes place in Chicago: four unknown assailants gun down five members of Bugs Moran's North Side Gang, rivals of the notorious Al Capone.

Racing driver Graham Hill, born on 15 February.

Friday 15: Racing driver Graham Hill is born in London, England (died 1975).

Saturday 16: The New York Stock Exchange suffers widespread losses following a warning against speculative loans by the Federal Reserve.

Sunday 17: Actress Patricia Routledge (*Keeping Up Appearances*) is born in Cheshire, England.

February 1929

Monday 18: Spy thriller writer Len Deighton (*The Ipcress File, Funeral in Berlin*) is born in London, England.

Tuesday 19: 5,000 homes are submerged in Brazil during the country's worst flooding in over four decades.

Wednesday 20: Actress Amanda Blake (Miss Kitty in *Gunsmoke*) is born in Buffalo, N.Y. (Died 1989).

Thursday 21: Douglas Fairbanks talks on screen for the first time, as the part-talkie *The Iron Mask* premieres in New York City.

Douglas Fairbanks appears in his first 'talkie', *The Iron Mask.*

Amanda Blake, born 20 February.

Friday 22: US President Calvin Coolidge makes his farewell address to the American public.

Saturday 23: The silent drama film *Wild Orchids*, starring Greta Garbo, is released.

Sunday 24: *Dagblad* newspaper in the Netherlands reveals details of the Franco-Belgian Accord, a secret military treaty between France and Belgium seen as threatening to the Dutch.

February/March 1929

Boxer Jack Dempsey.

Monday 25: A man breaks into the bedroom of boxing champion Jack Dempsey in Miami Beach, Florida and fires a revolver at Dempsey, who is unhurt. The assailant is never identified.

Tuesday 26: Grand Teton National Park in Wyoming is established.

Wednesday 27: Air ace Charles Lindbergh and his fiancée Anne Morrow escape serious injury when the plane Lindbergh is piloting overturns while landing at Mexico City.

Thursday 28: Police in Budapest, Hungary, arrest 60 people at the headquarters of the Communist Party, claiming they are part of a plot to overthrow the government.

Friday 1: France ratifies the anti-war Kellogg-Briand Pact.

Saturday 2: The San Francisco Bay toll bridge opens. At 12 miles long it is the longest bridge in the world at this date.

Sunday 3: Over 2000 people are reported to have died following extremely cold weather in Paris, France.

Charles Lindbergh and Anne Morrow.

March 1929

Monday 4: Herbert Hoover is inaugurated as the 31st President of the USA. It is the first such ceremony to be recorded by sound newsreels.

Tuesday 5: Gillis Grafström of Sweden wins the Men's Competition of the World Figure Skating Championships in London.

Wednesday 6: Turkey and Bulgaria sign a treaty of friendship.

President Hoover.

Thursday 7: Joe Davis wins his third world title at the World Snooker Championship in London.

Friday 8: Rebel troops in Mexico capture the city of Juárez in the country's Cristero Rebellion against enforced secularism.

Saturday 9: Charles Lindbergh flies from Mexico City to Brownsville, Texas, to inaugurate air mail services between the two cities.

Sunday 10: Mexican government forces attack rebel troops and seize the municipality of Cañitas.

Left: Cristero (pro-Catholic) rebels in Mexico.

March 1939

Sir Henry Seagrave.

The *Golden Arrow.*

Monday 11: Britain's Sir Henry Seagrave sets the world land speed record at 231 mph in his *Golden Arrow* car at Daytona Beach, Florida.

Tuesday 12: Mexican rebels retreat from Saltillo as President Emilio Portes Gil announces that the uprising has been defeated.

Wednesday 13: Leon Trotsky gives his first interview to the press while in exile in Turkey, announcing that he is writing a book about his opposition to Stalin.

Thursday 14: The town of Elba, Alabama, is submerged under ten feet of water as the Pea River floods.

Friday 15: Severe flooding spreads from Alabama to the states of Georgia and Florida.

Saturday 16: The musical film *Queen of the Night Clubs* starring Texas Guinan and George Raft is released.

Leon Trotsky.

Sunday 17: US pilot Mrs Louise Thaden sets the record for the longest female flight at 22 hours 3 minutes.

March 1929

Monday 18: Mexican President Emilio Portes Gil announces that peace negotiations have begun with troops involved in the recent Cristero Rebellion.

Tuesday 19: Martial arts expert Nam Tae Hi, known as 'the father of Vietnamese Taekwondo' is born in Seoul, Korea. (Died 2013).

Wednesday 20: France's Marshal Ferdinand Foch, supreme allied commander during the First World War, dies aged 77.

Marshall Foch.

Thursday 21: 46 miners are killed in an explosion at the Kinloch coal mine, Parnassus, Pennsylvania.

Friday 22: Comics artist Mort Drucker, for many years cover artist for *Mad* magazine, is born in Brooklyn, N.Y.

Saturday 23: Sir Roger Bannister, first man to run a mile in under four minutes, is born in Harrow, London. (died 2018).

Mussolini (centre) and his Fascists.

Sunday 24: Mussolini's National Fascist Party receives 98% of the vote in the Italian general election. Opposition parties are banned.

March 1929

Monday 25: 35 people are injured in crowd fighting over racist heckling when Jackie Fields defeats Jack Thompson to gain the world welterweight boxing title in Chicago.

Tuesday 26: Nearly two million people line the streets of Paris to view the funeral cortege of Marshal Foch en route to Notre Dame cathedral.

Wednesday 27: Gangster Al Capone appears before a grand jury in Chicago on bootlegging charges. He is arrested for contempt of court and bailed for $500.

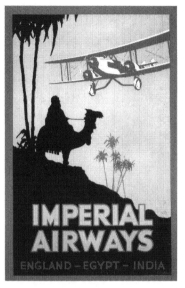

Imperial Airways India service poster.

Thursday 28: Japan agrees to withdraw occupying forces from Shandong, China.

Friday 29: The last major battle involving camel-mounted troops takes place at Sabilla in Arabia between Ikhwan rebels and the army of Ibn Saud.

Saturday 30: Imperial Airways begins its first regular service between London and Karachi in India (now Pakistan).

Al Capone.

Sunday 31: The aeroplane Southern Cross, piloted by Charles Kingsford Smith, goes missing while attempting to fly from Australia to England. The crew are found and rescued two weeks later but two men perish in the rescue attempt.

April 1929

Monday 1: Czech-French author Milan Kundera (*The Unbearable Lightness of Being*) is born in Brno, Czechoslovakia.

Tuesday 2: Two thirds of voters in Wisconsin vote in a referendum to loosen the state's prohibition laws to allow the sale of 2.75% beer.

Wednesday 3: Austrian Chancellor Ignaz Seipel resigns as his coalition government breaks down.

Carl Benz, inventor of the motor car.

Thursday 4: Carl Benz, German automotive pioneer widely accepted as the inventor of the automobile, dies aged 84.

The island of Heligoland, c.1890.

Friday 5: Actor Nigel Hawthorne (*Yes, Minister, The Madness of King George*) is born in Coventry, England (died 2001).

Saturday 6: Residents of the tiny German archipelago of Heligoland stage a demonstration demanding restoration of British rule, which ended in 1890.

Sunday 7: Austria defeats Italy 3-0 in the Central European International Cup. Italians accuse Austrians of foul play and complain that a sideways Hungarian flag was used to represent Italy.

Monday 8: Five people are wounded as Indian revolutionaries throw bombs into the colonial British Central Legislative Assembly building in New Delhi.

Tuesday 9: Pioneering New Zealand/Australian opthalmologist Fred Hollows is born in Dunedin, New Zealand (died 1993).

Wednesday 10: Swedish-French actor Max von Sydow (*The Seventh Seal, The Greatest Story Ever Told, Game of Thrones*) is born in Lund, Sweden.

Thursday 11: The crew of the *Southern Cross* aeroplane which disappeared near Sydney, Australia en route to England on 31 March, are found alive and well stranded on mudflats in northwestern Australia.

Max Von Sydow.

Friday 12: Arches National Park in Utah is named a National Monument.

Saturday 13: German Reichsbank President Hjalmar Schacht rejects Allied proposals for restructuring German war reparations payments.

Sunday 14: Britain's William Grover-Williams wins the first Monaco Grand Prix motor race.

William Grover-Williams in a Bugatti Type 35.

April 1929

Monday 15: Author J.M. Barrie signs over the royalties of his book *Peter Pan* in perpetuity to London's Great Ormond Street Hospital for Sick Children.

Tuesday 16: The French government revokes its permission to allow exiled controversial British occult writer Aleister Crowley to live there and gives him 24 hours to leave the country.

Wednesday 17: Baseball legend Babe Ruth marries Claire Merritt Hodgson in New York City.

Babe Ruth.

JM Barrie.

Thursday 18: British businessman and haulage magnate Eddie Stobart is born in Cumberland, England.

Friday 19: Canada's Johnny Miles wins the Boston Marathon.

Saturday 20: The first all-Fascist parliament opens in Italy.

Sunday 21: Six people are killed when a Maddux Airlines plane collides with a US army aircraft near San Diego, California.

April 1929

Monday 22: US President Herbert Hoover announces that crime is the nation's biggest problem, and warns that 'life and property are relatively more unsafe than in any other civilised country in the world.'

President Hoover on the radio.

Tuesday 23: Police in Romania arrest 35 communist party members suspected of plotting against the government.

Wednesday 24: Canada agrees to arbitration with the USA over compensation for the US coastguard's shelling and sinking of the Canadian bootlegging vessel *I'm Alone* in March.

Thursday 25: Tornadoes kill 40 people in Georgia and South Carolina.

Friday 26: The Royal Air Force completes the first non-stop flight from Britain to India. The flight, in a Fairey Long-range Monoplane, takes 50 hours 37 minutes.

Fairey Long-range Monoplane.

Saturday 27: Bolton Wanderers defeat Portsmouth 2-0 in the FA Cup Final at Wembley Stadium, London.

Sunday 28: 500 Mexican rebels surrender in Sonora as the Cristero rebellion draws to a close.

April/May 1929

Monday 29: The British Parliament debates the Marriage Bill which proposes to raise the minimum age of legal marriage (with parental consent) from 14 to 16 for boys and from 12 to 16 for girls.

Tuesday 30: Thorval Stauning becomes Prime Minister of Denmark for the second time.

Wednesday 1: 3,800 people are killed in the Koppeh Dagh earthquake in Iran and Turkmenistan.

Thursday 2: 42 people are killed when a tornado hits Rye Cove, Virginia.

The Marx Brothers.

Friday 3: The Marx Brothers' first full length film, *The Cocoanuts*, is released.

Laurel and Hardy.

Saturday 4: Comedy duo Laurel and Hardy release their first 'talkie', *Unaccustomed As We Are.* It includes Oliver Hardy's catchphrase 'Why don't you do something to help me?'

Sunday 5: 54 policemen are arrested for mutiny in Berlin, Germany, following four days of street battles with communists.

May 1929

Monday 6: Paul Lauterbur, Nobel prize winning chemist and pioneer of magnetic resonance imaging (MRI) scans, is born in Sidney, Ohio. (Died 2007).

Tuesday 7: During a dinner party, gangster Al Capone kills four fellow mobsters whom he accuses of treachery.

Wednesday 8: American author, psychic and medium Jane Roberts, aka 'Seth' is born in Albany, N.Y. (Died 1984).

Camilla Horn.

Thursday 9: The Ibero-American Exposition of 1929 opens in Seville, Spain.

Walter Hagen.

Friday 10: US golfer Walter Hagen wins the 64th Open Championship at Muirfield, Scotland.

Saturday 11: The romantic film *Eternal Love* starring John Barrymore and German actress Camilla Horn is released. It is Barrymore's last silent picture.

Sunday 12: Prohibition is rejected in Switzerland by almost two-thirds of voters in a national referendum.

May 1929

Monday 13: Gangsters from eight US states including Al Capone and Bugsy Siegel meet in Atlantic City, N.J., to form a national crime syndicate in full view of the media.

Tuesday 14: Canadian ice hockey player Gump Worsley is born in Montreal, Quebec (died 2007).

Wednesday 15: 123 people are killed when the Cleveland Clinic in Cleveland, Ohio, catches fire.

Thursday 16: The first Academy Awards (Oscars) ceremony is held in Los Angeles. The First World War drama *Wings*, starring Clara Bow and Gary Cooper, wins the Award for Best Picture.

Friday 17: Mobster Al Capone is arrested for carrying concealed weapons and sentenced to one year in prison.

Saturday 18: *Small Talk,* the first 'talkie' made by child comedy team Our Gang (aka The Little Rascals) is released.

Sunday 19: Two people are killed during a stampede for shelter when a downpour hits the Yankee Stadium in New York City during a baseball game.

War drama *Wings* wins the first Academy Award for Best Picture.

May 1929

The opening of the Council House, Nottingham.

Monday 20: The 1929 Barcelona International Exposition opens in Spain.

Tuesday 21: Sergei Prokofiev's ballet *The Prodigal Son* opens in Paris.

Wednesday 22: The iconic Council House, which includes a 10-tonne clock bell, opens in Nottingham, England.

Thursday 23: The first cartoon in which Mickey Mouse speaks, The *Karnival Kid*, is released.

Friday 24: The United Free Church of Scotland and the Church of Scotland agree to unite.

Saturday 25: Operatic soprano Beverly Sills is born in Brooklyn, New York.

Sunday 26: The monoplane *Fort Worth* sets a new record for the longest flight time, remaining in the air for over 172 hours, almost a full day longer than the aeroplane *Question Mark* in January.

Russian composer Sergei Prokofiev.

May/June 1929

Monday 27: Aviator Charles Lindbergh and Anne Morrow are married in a surprise ceremony near Englewood, New Jersey.

Tuesday 28: *On With the Show*, the first all talking, all colour film premieres in New York City.

Wednesday 29: One person is killed during a series of sewer explosions in Ottawa, Canada.

Thursday 30: The general election in Britain results in a hung parliament (no overall majority for any party).

Friday 31: The Ford Motor Company signs a nine year contract with the Soviet Union, agreeing to help build a factory in Nizhny Novgorod.

President Sun Yat-sen.

Saturday 1: In an elaborate ceremony, the remains of Sun Yat-sen, first President of the Republic of China, are moved from Beijing and re-buried in the Sun Yat sen Mausoleum in Nanjing.

Sunday 2: 18 countries sign an agreement in London for unified safety regulations for ships at sea, including the requirement to carry sufficient lifeboats for all passengers.

June 1929

Monday 3: Actors Douglas Fairbanks Jr. and Joan Crawford are married in New York.

Tuesday 4: British Prime Minister Stanley Baldwin resigns. He is replaced by Labour's Ramsey MacDonald.

Wednesday 5: Pope Pius XI attacks Italian leader Benito Mussolini as 'heretical' over Mussolini's recent anti-Christian statements.

Thursday 6: The Westlake Exposition world's fair opens in Hangzhou, Republic of China.

Friday 7: The Lateran Treaty goes into effect, making the Vatican City an independent state within Italy.

Saturday 8: Britain's new Prime Minister, Ramsay MacDonald, makes his first radio broadcast, in which he stresses the need for international disarmament.

Sunday 9: Western movie star Louis Bennison is found dead with actress Margaret Lawrence following an apparent murder-suicide.

Mr Ramsey MacDonald, Britain's new Prime Minister.

June 1929

Monday 10: Pope Pius XI promulgates 21 articles which lay out the basic laws of the Vatican City.

Tuesday 11: William Dickson Boyce, founder of the Boy Scouts of America, dies aged 70.

Wednesday 12: The war film *The Four Feathers*, starring William Powell and Fay Wray, premieres in New York City.

Thursday 13: James H. Snook, a professor at Ohio State University, murders student Theora Hix following a three-year affair; the trial later causes a media sensation.

Friday 14: The National Party led by JBM Hertzog wins the South African general election.

Saturday 15: US President Hoover signs the Agricultural Marketing Act into law. Known as the 'farm relief bill' it is intended to promote agricultural commodities in interstate and foreign commerce.

General Bramwell Booth, leader of the Salvation Army.

Sunday 16: Bramwell Booth, second General of the Salvation Army and son of its founder William Booth, dies aged 73.

Monday 17: Seven people are killed when an Imperial Airways Handley Page W10 aircraft crashes in the English Channel en route from London to Paris; six passengers survive.

Tuesday 18: The US Reapportionment Act 1929 is passed, limiting the size of the US House of Representatives.

Wednesday 19: Actress Thelma Barlow, famous for her role as Mavis Wilton in long running TV soap opera *Coronation Street*, is born in Middlesborough, England.

Thursday 20: Brawling breaks out in the Argentinian parliament during a debate over the dismissal of government employees; inkwells are hurled and two members agree to a duel the following day.

Friday 21: The government of Mexico makes peace with the Vatican, agreeing to revise its anti-clerical policies and allow churches to re-open.

Saturday 22: Spanish aviator Ramon Franco goes missing near the Azores during a transatlantic flight attempt.

Sunday 23: The French city of Verdun holds a celebration of its reconstruction following heavy damage in the First World War.

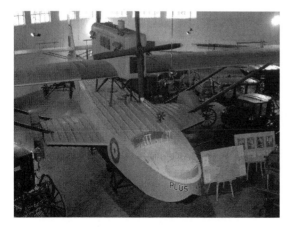

Ramon Franco's seaplane *Plus Ultra*, now a museum exhibit in Buenos Aires, Argentina.

June 1929

Monday 24: Thousands of Londoners line the streets of the British capital for the funeral procession of General Bramwell Booth, leader of the Salvation Army.

Tuesday 25: US President Hoover signs the Boulder Canyon Project Act, authorising $165 million for the construction of the Boulder Dam.

Wednesday 26: Japan ratifies the Kellog-Briand anti-war pact.

Thursday 27: Colour television images are demonstrated at Bell Laboratories in New York.

Friday 28: Radical English poet and philosopher Edward Carpenter *(right)* dies aged 84.

Saturday 29: Aviator Ramon Franco and his crew are found alive floating off the coast of the Azores, a week after going missing during their transatlantic flight attempt.

Sunday 30: Britain's William Grover-Williams wins the French Grand Prix.

William Grover-Williams wins a motor race.

Monday 1: Britain and China sign a pact in which Britain pledges to help build China's navy.

Tuesday 2: Imelda Marcos, wife of Phillipines president Ferdinand Marcos, is born in Manila.

Wednesday 3: Britain's new Labour government announces it will cut imports and promote British manufacturing as much as possible to boost employment.

Thursday 4: Veteran classical pianist Max Olding is born in Australia.

Friday 5: British police seize twelve paintings of nudes by DH Lawrence from a London gallery on grounds of indecency.

Saturday 6: France's Henri Cochet defeats Jean Borotra in the tennis Men's Singles Final at Wimbledon.

Henri Cochet.

Sunday 7: A day of prayer and thanksgiving is observed in churches across the British Empire for the recovery of HM King George V *(left)* from a long illness.

July 1929

Monday 8: Germany opens its first major aviation museum in Stuttgart, on the ninety-first anniversary of the birth of Count Ferdinand von Zeppelin, inventor of the Zeppelin airship.

Tuesday 9: 24 men are killed when two British submarines HMS *H47* and HMS *L12* collide off the coast of Wales.

The *Southern Cross*.

Wednesday 10: The *Southern Cross* aeroplane sets a new record by flying from Australia to England in just under 13 days, more than two days faster than the record set in February 1928.

Thursday 11: Britain's Labour government refuses to grant political asylum to Leon Trotsky.

Friday 12: A new flight endurance record is set as the Buhl Airsedan *Angeleno* lands after more than ten days in the air over California.

Saturday 13: Germany agrees to pay 500 million gold marks to Belgium to compensate for useless German currency left in the country following the German occupation in the First World War.

Sunday 14: The Soviet Union gives China a three day ultimatum to release Russian officials arrested during a Chinese takeover of the Eastern Railway on the Soviet border.

July 1929

Monday 15: HM King George V undergoes a major operation to treat a lung abscess.

Tuesday 16: China gives a counter-ultimatum to the Soviet Union in the Chinese Eastern Railway crisis, calling for the release of 1000 Chinese nationals.

Wednesday 17: The Soviet Union breaks off diplomatic relations with China and mobilises troops on the Russo-Chinese border.

Thursday 18: Rhythm and blues musician Screamin' Jay Hawkins is born in Cleveland, Ohio (died 2000).

Friday 19: The League of Nations, forerunner of the United Nations, ends its eight day enquiry session into the future of British Mandatory Palestine (now Israel).

Screamin' Jay Hawkins, (*I Put a Spell on You*) is born in Cleveland, Ohio.

Saturday 20: 2000 people are left homeless after a fire destroys the old quarter of Ankara, Turkey.

Sunday 21: The French government agrees to the Mellon-Berenger agreement on war debt repayments to the USA. The agreement is deeply unpopular with those who believe the debt should be waived in light of France's sacrifice.

July 1929

Monday 22: The Sino-Soviet Conflict begins as Russian troops being firing into Chinese territory near Pogranichny.

Tuesday 23: The Soviet Union and China agree to meet for peace talks.

Wednesday 24: The Rt Hon the Lord Lloyd, British High Commissioner in Egypt, resigns following differences of opinion with Foreign Secretary Arthur Henderson.

Thursday 25: Huge crowds gather to see Pope Pius XI make the first public appearance of a pope in Rome since 1870. Popes had refused to leave the Vatican City until their legal status was resolved by the Lateran Treaty in February 1929.

Friday 26: France's Prime Minister Raymond Poincare resigns due to ill health.

Saturday 27: The Geneva Convention on the treatment of prisoners of war is signed in Geneva, Switzerland.

Sunday 28: Jacqueline Kennedy Onassis, First Lady of the USA, is born in Southampton, NY (died 1994).

Pope Pius XI.

Jackie Kennedy Onassis.

July/August 1929

Monday 29: 500,000 cotton workers in 1500 British mills go on strike in protest over their wages being cut by 12.5 per cent.

Tuesday 30: The world flight endurance record is extended by a full week as a Curtiss Robin lands after spending over 17 days in the air over Missouri.

Wednesday 31: Long running American children's magazine *The Youth's Companion,* first published in 1827, ceases to exist as it merges with *The American Boy* magazine.

Fats Waller.

Thursday 1: 300,000 people participate in an anti-war demonstration in Berlin on the fifteenth anniversary of the outbreak of the First World War.

Friday 2: Fats Waller records his hit song *Ain't Misbehavin'.*

Saturday 3: Norwegian-American economist Thorstein Veblen, author of seminal work *The Theory of the Leisure Class*, dies aged 72.

Sunday 4: The *Graf Zeppelin* airship completes its third transatlantic flight as it lands in Lakenhurst, New Jersey.

The airship *Graf Zeppelin.*

August 1929

Monday 5: British suffragette and union leader Dame Millicent Fawcett GBE dies aged 82.

Tuesday 6: Great Britain signs a treaty with Egypt ending British occupation, replacing it with a military alliance and rights to station troops along the Suez Canal.

Dame Millicent Fawcett GBE as a young woman.

Wednesday 7: Colombia's Antioquia Railway is finally completed after 55 years of construction.

Thursday 8: Fighting between Jews and Arabs takes place in British Mandatory Palestine following a dispute about construction near to the sacred Western Wall in Jerusalem.

Friday 9: Two people are killed during clashes with police and communist demonstrators in Berlin, Germany.

Saturday 10: Fiendish oriental villain Dr Fu Manchu makes his American film debut in the talkie *The Mysterious Dr Fu Manchu*, played by Warner Oland who went on to star as detective Charlie Chan.

Sunday 11: Baseball legend Babe Ruth hits the 500th major league home run of his career.

August 1939

Monday 12: Hungarian police arrest 13 people suspected of involvement in a poisoning ring centred on the village of Nagyrév.

Tuesday 13: At a conference in the Hague, the Allies agree to reduce the number of troops occupying the Rhineland by 1 September.

Wednesday 14: Ohio State University professor James H. Snook is convicted of murdering his mistress, student Theora Hix, and sentenced to death by electrocution.

Thursday 15: British cotton workers, on strike since the end of July, agree to resume work at pre-strike wages.

Friday 16: Muslim looters attack a synagogue in Jerusalem as the violent dispute over property rights at the Wailing Wall continues.

Saturday 17: U2 spy pilot Gary Powers, captured by the Soviets in 1960, is born in Jenkins, Kentucky.

Sunday 18: 20 pilots compete in the first all-female air race, the Women's Air Derby, from California to Ohio.

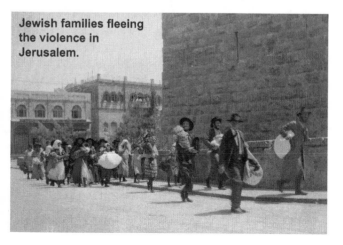
Jewish families fleeing the violence in Jerusalem.

August 1929

Monday 19: The first and only successful metal-skinned airship, the US Navy's *ZMC-2*, is launched at Lakenhurst, NJ.

Tuesday 20: The first major film with an all-black cast, *Hallelujah*, directed by King Vidor, premieres in the USA.

Wednesday 21: Mahatma Gandhi is elected president of the Indian National Congress, but declines to accept the post.

Thursday 22: General Otto Liman von Sanders, senior German commander in the near-east theatre during the First World War, dies aged 74.

Friday 23: Six days of rioting and violence between Muslims and Jews begins in Jerusalem. Over 300 people are killed, some by British troops attempting to restore order.

Saturday 24: Martial law is declared in Jerusalem as around 70 Jews are massacred by Muslims in Hebron.

Sunday 25: A public address system is used for the first time at a baseball game when the New York Giants play the Pittsburgh Pirates. The system does not become widespread until the 1940s.

A synagogue desecrated during rioting in Hebron.

August/September 1929

Monday 26: The *Graf Zeppelin* airship arrives in Los Angeles, completing the first non-stop trans-Pacific flight.

Tuesday 27: 43 members of the Sicilian Mafia are sent to prison following a mass trial.

Wednesday 28: In an interview for the *Christian Century* newspaper, Albert Einstein states 'science without religion is lame, religion without science is blind.'

Thursday 29: The *Graf Zeppelin* airship completes a round the world trip at Lakehurst, NJ, taking 21 days with three stops.

Albert Einstein.

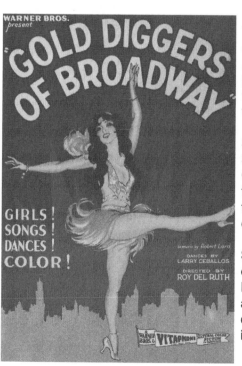

Friday 30: The Technicolor musical comedy film *Gold Diggers of Broadway* premieres; it goes on to become a worldwide hit.

Saturday 31: The Soviet Union accepts Chinese proposals for the settlement of the Sino-Soviet conflict.

Sunday 1: A bomb explodes in the Berlin Reichstag at 4.00 am; damage is caused but nobody is injured.

September 1929

Monday 2: The Grand Mufti of Jerusalem, Haj Amin-al-Husseini *(left)*, warns that Palestine cannot regain peace unless Britain abandons its policy of making the region a Jewish homeland.

Tuesday 3: Owen Thomas Edgar, the last surviving US veteran of the Mexican-American War (1846-48) dies aged 98.

Wednesday 4: 17 people are killed when a bomb factory explodes in Brescia, Italy.

Thursday 5: US comedian and actor Bob Newhart *(right)* is born in Oak Park, Illinois.

Friday 6: Leading South African clothing retail chain Edgars is founded in Johannesburg.

Saturday 7: Britain's Richard Waghorn wins the 1929 Schneider Trophy air race, setting a new world flying speed record of 328.6 mph.

Sunday 8: Actress Patsy Ruth Miller (Esmerelda in *The Hunchback of Notre Dame*) marries director Tay Garnett in California.

Richard Waghorn *(far left)* with Great Britain's 1929 Schneider Trophy team.

September 1929

Monday 9: French Prime Minister Aristide Briand hosts a meeting on European unity for 28 nations, at which he declares 'We have laid the cornerstone of a European confederation'.

Tuesday 10: Britain's AH Oriebar breaks Richard Waghorn's air speed world record set on 7 September, reaching 355.8 mph.

Wednesday 11: Soviet troops push 40 miles into Chinese territory at Pogranichny.

Aristide Briand.

Thursday 12: The musical drama film *The Great Gabbo*, starring Erich von Stroheim, premieres in New York City.

Friday 13: Blues singer Bessie Smith releases *Nobody Knows You're When You're Down and Out.*

Saturday 14: British troops begin their withdrawal from the Rhineland in Germany, occupied since the end of the First World War.

Sunday 15: Seven men are arrested for the fatal shooting of union organiser Ella Mae Wiggins during a strike at Loray Mill, Gastonia, North Carolina, the previous day.

Blues singer Bessie Smith.

September 1929

Monday 16: The USA and Britain invite Japan, France and Italy to a naval disarmament conference scheduled for January 1930.

Mel Stewart.

Tuesday 17: Damage estimated at $3m is caused when wildfires hit oil company buildings in Ventura County, California.

Wednesday 18: US President Herbert Hoover makes a radio broadcast on peace and international arms reduction, calling for an end to 'the hate and fear which flows from the rivalry in building warships.'

Thursday 19: US actor Mel Stewart (*All in the Family, The Scarecrow and Mrs King*) is born in Cleveland, Ohio (died 2002).

Friday 20: 22 people are killed in a fire at the Study Club, a 'speakeasy' selling bootleg alcohol in Detroit, Michigan.

Saturday 21: Legendary Hungarian footballer Sándor Kocsis, one of the Golden Team or 'mighty Magyars' who defeated England 6-3 at Wembley in 1953, is born in Budapest (died 1979).

Joseph Goebbels.

Sunday 22: Berlin police arrest senior Nazi party member Joseph Goebbels after he allegedly fires shots at protestors during an anti-Nazi rally.

September 1929

Monday 23: Nobel Prize winning Austrian chemist Richard Adolf Zsigmondy dies aged 64.

Tuesday 24: German nationalists denounce the Allies' Young Plan for wartime reparations as 'flagrant dishonesty' during a rally attended by 20,000 people in Berlin.

Wednesday 25: Actor, writer and comedian Ronnie Barker (*The Two Ronnies, Porridge, Open All Hours*) is born in Bedford, England (died 2005).

Thursday 26: Jack Sharkey knocks out Tommy Loughran at Yankee Stadium to win boxing's American Heavyweight title.

Friday 27: Ernest Hemingway's First World War novel *A Farewell to Arms* is published.

Saturday 28: German nationalists submit a bill to their Interior Minister calling for a referendum against the Allied war reparations demands in the Young Plan.

Sunday 29: French pilots Dieudonné Costes and Maurice Bellonte set a world record by flying 5000 miles non-stop from Paris to Tsitsihar, China, in a Breguet 19 aeroplane.

Dieudonné Costes and Maurice Bellonte.

September/October 1929

Monday 30: The first rocket propelled plane, the RAK 1 piloted by Fritz von Opel, makes a test flight in Germany.

Tuesday 1: Britain restores diplomatic relations with the Soviet Union.

Wednesday 2: The historical 'talkie' *Disraeli*, starring George Arliss as Britain's nineteenth century Prime Minister Benjamin Disraeli, premieres in New York City.

Thursday 3: The Kingdom of Serbs, Croats and Slovenes changes its name to the Kingdom of Yugoslavia.

Friday 4: Ramsay MacDonald becomes the first sitting British Prime inester to visit the USA when he meets President Herbert Hoover in Washington, DC.

Saturday 5: Ramsay MacDonald and Herbert Hoover engage in disarmament talks at Rapidan Camp, Virginia.

Sunday 6: Nick Altrock (53) of the Washington Senators becomes one of only four men in major league baseball's history to score a hit when aged over 50.

Nick Altrock.

October 1929

Monday 7: 44 people are killed when the Norwegian passenger ship *Haakon VII* sinks off the Norwegian coast near Florø.

Tuesday 8: Ralph Capone, brother of mobster Al Capone, is arrested by US federal authorities for tax fraud.

Wednesday 9: The musical stage play *June Moon* directed by George S Kaufman opens on Broadway. It goes on to be broadcast as a radio play in 1940 starring Orson Welles and Jack Benny.

Thursday 10: The forces of Nadir Khan seize the city of Kabul in the Afghan Civil War.

Friday 11: The US Senate eases censorship laws on non-illustrated obscene books; the law is revoked in 1930.

Saturday 12: Comedian Harold Lloyd's first 'talkie', *Welcome Danger*, is released.

Sunday 13: The ocean liner RMS *Empress of Canada* runs aground off Vancouver Island; all passengers are safely evacuated.

Above: Harold Lloyd. Left: George S Kaufman.

October 1929

The *R101* airship.

Monday 14: Traffic in London comes to a standstill as crowds watch the British airship *R101* make its maiden voyage.

Tuesday 15: American economist Irving Fisher announces that stock prices have reached 'what looks like a permanently high plateau' and thathe expects prices to rise even further.

Wednesday 16: The British government compromises with coal mining unions' demands for a seven hour working day by offering a seven and a half hour day.

Thursday 17: British Prime Minister Ramsay MacDonald arrives in Canada to meet Prime Minister William Lyon Mackenzie King.

Friday 18: Britain's Privy Council grants women the right to be appointed the Canadian Senate, a victory for a group of Alberta women known as the Famous Five.

Saturday 19: The New York Stock Exchange (which opens on Saturday mornings until 1952) posts large losses amid a wave of selling.

Sunday 20: Two people are killed during violent protests in Berlin against the Allies' Young Plan for wartime reparations.

October 1929

Monday 21: Science fiction and fantasy writer Ursula K. Le Guin (author of the *Earthsea* series) is born in Berkeley, California (died 2018).

Tuesday 22: US National City Bank chairman Charles E. Mitchell declares recent losses on the stock market as 'a healthy reaction, which has probably overrun itself.'

Wednesday 23: An assassination attempt is made on Italy's Crown Prince Umberto at a wreath-laying ceremony in Brussels; the assailant is arrested immediately.

Thursday 24: Black Thursday: the beginning of the Wall Street Crash of 1929. A deluge of panic selling begins in the morning although this is temporarily shored up by the afternoon.

Friday 25: 21 men are executed for anti-government activities in Krasnodar in the Soviet Union.

Saturday 26: Transport authorities in London announce that all buses will be painted red, following unsuccessful trials of other colour schemes.

Sunday 27: In Rome, fascist leader Benito Mussolini addresses 60,000 blackshirts to commemorate the seventh anniversary of the March on Rome.

Cleaning up the New York Stock Exchange after the Wall Street Crash.

October/November 1929

Monday 28: Black Monday: the US stock market drops 12.82%, the biggest single-day fall in the history of the Dow Jones Industrial Average until 1987.

Tuesday 29: Black Tuesday: the US stock market falls another 11.73% as all hope of a quick recovery disappears. Sellers outnumber buyers ten to one and a record 16.4 million shares are exchanged.

Wednesday 30: US oil tycoon John D Rockefeller makes a rare public statement, announcing his belief that 'the fundamental conditions of the country are sound.'

John D Rockefeller.

Thursday 31: The Viceroy of India, Lord Irwin (later the Earl of Halifax), controversially announces that India should be granted semi-autonomous status as a British Dominion, similar to that of Canada and Australia.

Friday 1: The New York Stock Exchange closes for one day to correct book-keeping errors made during the rushed sales of the past few days.

**Lord Irwin,
Viceroy of India.**

Saturday 2: André Tardieu becomes the 97th Prime Minister of France.

Sunday 3: Habibullah Kalakani, the overthrown Emir of Afghanistan, is executed by firing squad.

November 1929

Monday 4: The Dow Jones Industrial Average falls a further 5.79%, ending hopes for a 'buying frenzy' as stock prices fall.

Tuesday 5: The British House of Commons votes 324-199 to recognise the Soviet Union.

Wednesday 6: The large German transport plane the Junkers G.38 makes its first flight from Dessau. Unusually, the plane includes passenger seating space inside its wings.

Thursday 7: New York's Museum of Modern Art opens.

Friday 8: James J. Riordan, president of the US County Trust Company, shoots himself after becoming distraught after the Wall Street Crash. It is one of the most widely publicised suicides of investors following the downturn.

Saturday 9: Chinese media reports that Soviet troops have crossed the Amur River near Blagoveshchensk; at the same time, severe fighting takes place in Hunan Province between communist and nationalist Chinese troops.

Sunday 10: The Harvard Economic Society announces 'a serious depression...is outside the range of probability.'

Soviet troops display banners captured from the Chinese.

November 1929

Monday 11: The Ambassador Bridge, connecting Detroit, Michigan, with Windsor, Ontario, Canada, is opened.

Tuesday 12: Actress and Princess of Monaco, Grace Kelly, is born in Philadelphia, Pennsylvania (died 1982).

Wednesday 13: The Wall Street Crash finally bottoms out with the Dow Jones Industrial Average closing at 198.69 points, only 52% of its September value.

Grace Kelly.

Thursday 14: Italy's fascist government seizes two large estates in Arezzo and Taranto, claiming the owners had failed to properly cultivate the land.

Friday 15: US President Herbert Hoover announces a conference of the nation's business leaders to discuss the economic measures required following the Wall Street Crash.

Saturday 16: Peter Boizot MBE, British entrepreneur and founder of the Pizza Express restaurant chain, is born in Peterborough, England.

Sunday 17: 19 people are killed in rioting during the election of Mexico's new President, Pascual Ortiz Rubio.

The Ambassador Bridge.

November 1929

Monday 18: 28 people are killed when a tsunami caused by the offshore Grand Banks earthquake hits Newfoundland; it remains the worst earthquake-related disaster in Canadian history.

Tuesday 19: The musical comedy film *The Love Parade* starring Maurice Chevalier and Jeanette Macdonald premieres in New York City.

Wednesday 20: Spanish surrealist painter Salvador Dali opens his first one-man Paris show.

Thursday 21: French troops begin withdrawal from the German city of Koblenz, occupied by them since the end of the First World War.

Friday 22: The government of the Soviet Union announces that any Soviet citizens living or working abroad who refuse an order to return home will be considered guilty of treason and executed once found.

Salvador Dali.

Saturday 23: US President Hoover asks all state governors to increase civil works programmes to create employment.

Sunday 24: The Soviet Union announces via radio its terms for cessation of hostilities with China, including the release of all imprisoned Soviet citizens and the withdrawal of Chinese forces from border areas.

November/December 1929

Monday 25: Two men are found guilty of obscenity in Cambridge, Massachusetts, for selling copies of D.H. Lawrence's novel *Lady Chatterley's Lover*.

Tuesday 26: The Chinese government appeals to the League of Nations (forerunner of the United Nations) for the Soviet Union to be punished for its acts of aggression in Manchuria.

Wednesday 27: The ocean liner RMS *Mauretania* collides with a ferry off the coast near New York, sinking the ferry and causing major damage to the *Mauretania*.

RMS *Mauretania.*

Thursday 28: US explorer Richard E. Byrd and three crew make the first aeroplane flight over the South Pole.

Friday 29: Germany's foreign minister Julius Curtis announces that Germany will meet the war reparations demanded by the allies in the Young Plan.

Saturday 30: Allied troops withdraw from the Koblenz region of Germany.

Sunday 1: Seven people are killed in a coal mine explosion in West Frankfort, Illinois.

December 1929

Monday 2: US President Herbert Hoover calls on the Soviet Union and China to end armed hostilities.

Tuesday 3: President Herbert Hoover makes his first State of the Union address, in which he states 'a special effort shall be made to expand construction work in order to assist in equalizing other deficits in employment.'

Wednesday 4: Former British Prime Minister David Lloyd George announces in Parliament that war is inevitable without disarmament, criticising the ineffectiveness of the League of Nations.

Thursday 5: The King of Italy, Victor Emmanuel III and Queen Elena visit the Pope, the first time the sovereign of unified Italy enters the Vatican.

Friday 6: Turkish women receive the right to vote.

David Lloyd George.

Saturday 7: King Faisal I of Iraq, a promoter of Muslim-Jewish co-operation, declares his support for Britain's plans for a Jewish homeland in Palestine, but says it should not become a Jewish state.

Sunday 8: The Nazi party receives 11.3% of the vote in state elections in Thuringia, Germany; a marked increase from the 2.6% received in national elections the previous year.

King Faisal I.

December 1929

Monday 9: Bob Hawke, 23rd Prime Minister of Australia, is born in Bordertown, South Australia.

Tuesday 10: Author Thomas Mann (*Death in Venice*) receives the Nobel Prize for Literature.

Wednesday 11: Eight convicts and a warden are killed during rioting at Auburn Prison, New York.

Thursday 12: The last British troops occupying the German Rhineland are withdrawn.

Friday 13: Canadian actor Christopher Plummer (Georg von Trapp in *The Sound of Music*) is born in Toronto, Ontario.

Bob Hawke, former Prime Minister of Australia, born on 9 December.

Saturday 14: Alexandros Zaimis is elected as President of Greece.

Sunday 15: Pope Pius XI beatifies 136 English martyrs who were hanged during the Reformation.

Christopher Plummer, star of *The Sound of Music*, born on 13 February.

December 1929

Monday 16: The British airship *R100*, sister vessel to the *R101*, makes its maiden flight. The design team includes Barnes Wallis, later famous for inventing the Bouncing Bomb, and engineer Nevil Shute, who goes on to enjoy a successful career as a novelist.

Tuesday 17: 61 people are killed in an explosion in a coal mine at McAlester, Oklahoma.

Wednesday 18: The cruise ship RMS *Fort Victoria* sinks after a collision with the ocean liner SS *Algonquin* off the coast of New York; all hands are rescued.

Thursday 19: Two people are killed during rioting by the unemployed in Berlin, Germany.

Friday 20: Pope Pius XI becomes the first pope since 1870 to celebrate mass outside the Vatican, in the Archbasilica of St John Lateran. Previous Popes had remained in the Vatican due to a political dispute with the government.

Joseph Stalin.

Saturday 21: The entire issue of this day's *Pravda* newspaper in Russia is devoted to adulatory articles about Soviet premier Joseph Stalin following his fiftieth birthday on Wednesday.

Sunday 22: Germany holds a referendum on whether to accept the Young Plan for war reparations or not; only a small percentage of voters turn out and the result (to not accept the plan) is deemed invalid.

December 1929

Monday 23: An assassination attempt is made on the Viceroy of India, Lord Irwin, when a bomb is thrown into his railway carriage in Delhi; he escapes unhurt.

Tuesday 24: The most serious fire at the White House takes place since it was burnt by the British in 1814. The West Wing is severely damaged and many important documents are lost.

Wednesday 25: One of the most expensive part-colour musical films to this date, *Hit the Deck*, starring Jack Oakie and Polly Walker, premieres in Los Angeles.

Thursday 26: Pope Pius XI recieves Italian royalty and nobility at the Vatican as a gesture of goodwill marking the restoration of cordial relations between the papacy and the Italian state.

Friday 27: The Soviet ambassador to Britain states that the USSR will refrain from communist agitation in the British Dominions.

Saturday 28: Nine people are killed when police fire on pro-independence demonstrators in the New Zealand-administered island of Samoa.

Sunday 29: Following movements towards partial independence for India via Dominion status, the Indian National Congress calls for complete independence from British rule.

Monday 30: The musical revue *Wake Up and Dream* by Cole Porter opens on Broadway.

Tuesday 31: US Secretary of Commerce Robert P Lamont announces that unemployment is 'hardly more than is usual' and that 'during the coming year the country will make steady progress'.

Birthday Notebooks
...a great alternative to a card.

Handy 60 page ruled notebooks with a significant event from the year heading each page.

Available from Montpelier Publishing at Amazon.

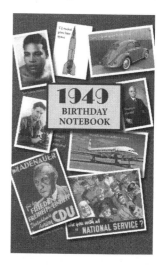